I0012612

The content of this work is protected by law, which proves penalties of imprisonment and/or fines, as well as compensation for damages, for those who reproduce, plagiarize, distribute, or publicly communicate, in whole or in part, a literary, artistic, or scientific work without authorization. Furthermore, all rights reserved and unauthorized use is prohibited. The work is protected nationally and internationally, and any modification or adaptation requires prior written authorization.

© First edition: June 2023
Luis Angel Perez Fernandez
luisangel0165@td506-cr.com
ISBN: 9798850286507

"I want to express my deep gratitude to my entire family for their unconditional support throughout all my projects and goals in life. Thank you for always believing in me and for being by my side every step of the way."

Warning:

Before delving into the pages of this book, it is important to highlight that it is not an exhaustive course in artificial intelligence (AI), but rather an accessible and understandable explanation of what AI is and how it influences our world. The main goal of this book is to supply an overview of AI, addressing its fundamental concepts and its various applications in different areas.

I want you to become familiar with the basic principles of AI and understand its transformative potential in society. However, it is relevant to note that this book is not the only resource needed to delve into the subject. I recommend using it as a starting point, to understand the basics of AI and then complement your learning with other resources, specialized courses and practical projects.

In this way, you will be able to develop concrete skills in the implementation and application of AI in your area of interest. Remember that AI is a constantly evolving and learning field, and my goal is to provide you with a clear and solid introduction to its essential concepts.

Enjoy reading and delve into the wonders and challenges that await us in the fascinating world of artificial intelligence!

CONTENT:

Preface:

Welcome to "The Universe of Artificial Intelligence: Exploring Its Basics". This book invites you to delve into the fascinating world of Artificial Intelligence (AI) and discover the essential fundamentals that drive this revolutionary discipline. Artificial Intelligence has been a topic of interest for decades.

Its origin dates to the 50s, when computer pioneers began to wonder if machines could be programmed to think and solve problems similarly to humans. It was then that the field of AI study appeared, with the aim of developing systems that could simulate human intelligence.

Over the years, AI has seen significant advances. In the beginning, researchers focused on developing logic programs and specific rules so that machines could perform specific tasks. However, these approaches proved to be limited, as they could not adapt to new situations or learn from experience.

It was in the 1980s that another focus on AI appeared: machine learning. This perspective allowed machines to learn from data and improve their performance as more information was provided to them. Through learning algorithms, machines could recognize patterns, make predictions and make decisions based on available information. In recent years, deep learning has been one of the biggest advances in the field of AI. Based on artificial neural networks, deep learning has proven to be highly effective in image recognition, natural language processing, and other complex tasks. These neural networks are inspired by the workings of the human brain, with interconnected layers of nodes that process information hierarchically. Today, AI is found everywhere, from search engines and social media to self-driving cars and healthcare, AI is transforming the way we live and work. With advances such as natural language processing and computer vision, machines can understand and communicate with humans more naturally, opening a world of possibilities in human-machine interaction.

This book has the main basic concepts of AI and its definition. Throughout its pages, we will understand how AI has evolved over time, from its theoretical beginnings to its practical application in different fields. How it has become a powerful tool capable of analyzing substantial amounts of data, recognizing patterns, making intelligent decisions, and solving complex problems.

We'll delve into the world of machine learning and algorithms, to understand how these techniques allow machines to learn from data and improve their performance over time.

We will explore concepts such as supervised learning, unsupervised learning, and reinforcement learning, understanding how each of them contributes to empowering machines to perform specific tasks. In addition to the fascinating field of neural networks and deep learning.

We'll discover how these technologies are revolutionizing areas like computer vision and natural language processing.

We will see how machines can recognize objects in images, understand the meaning behind a text and even generate original content. Also, the processing of natural language and its application in the creation of chatbots and virtual assistants increasingly sophisticated. How machines can intelligently understand and generate text, opening new possibilities in human-machine communication.

In the realm of computer vision, we will explore how machines can "see" and understand images and videos. We will get to know the algorithms and techniques used in this field and explore successful cases in different industries, such as medicine, security and entertainment industry. Finally, we will reflect on the ethical challenges associated with the development and use of AI. We will discuss the important considerations we need to consider when creating and applying AI systems and contemplate the ethical future of this ever-evolving discipline. We will discuss topics such as algorithmic bias, data privacy, and accountability in automated decision-making.

In short, this book will take you on an exciting journey through the vast universe of Artificial Intelligence.

I hope you enjoy exploring the basics and find inspiration in the possibilities AI offers for the future of technology and society. Let's start this adventure together!

Chapter 1: Introduction to Artificial Intelligence

In this first chapter, we will take the first steps in the field of artificial intelligence. We will explore the fundamentals that will allow us to understand what AI is and how it is affecting our lives in surprising ways.

We'll start by exploring the definition and basics of AI. We want to discover how AI looks to create machines capable of performing tasks that require human intelligence, speech recognition, decision making, and learning. In addition, we will dive into key terms of algorithms, machine learning models and neural networks, which are the basis of how AI works.

Next, we will delve into the practical applications of AI in our daily lives. We will see how AI is present in our interactions with virtual assistants, in our smartphones, in movie and product recommendation systems, and in facial recognition applications. We will discover how AI has been integrated into many aspects of our routine, improving our efficiency and providing innovative solutions.

Finally, we'll explore how AI is transforming various industries. We will look at how AI is revolutionizing sectors such as medicine, agriculture, coordination and trade. We will learn about real use cases in which AI drives efficiency, improving accuracy and enabling more informed decision-making in these fields.

This chapter will give us a solid overview of AI, from its fundamentals to its impact on our daily lives and different industries. Get ready to discover how AI is changing the way we live, work and relate to the world around us.

- Definition and basic concepts of AI

Artificial Intelligence (AI) is a fascinating field of study and development that focuses on creating systems and programs capable of conducting tasks that require human skills, such as learning, reasoning, belief, and decision making. Over time, AI has undergone significant evolution since its earliest concepts.

Initially, AI focused on developing programs and algorithms that were more efficient than humans at solving specific problems. These systems were based on predefined rules, where logical instructions were set up to make decisions or perform specific tasks. However, these systems were limited and required extensive programming to cover all possible scenarios.

With the advancement of research and technology, AI has bought new capabilities and diversified its approaches. One of the most prominent approaches is machine learning, which allows machines to learn from data and improve its performance without explicit programming. Using algorithms that analyze patterns in the data and adjust their models, machines can make predictions and decisions more accurately.

An important milestone in the evolution of AI has been the development of artificial neural networks, which are inspired by the functioning of the human brain. These networks are made up of layers of interconnected nodes, allowing them to process information and extract complex features from data. For example, convolutional neural networks are widely used in computer vision to recognize objects in images.

Currently, AI has expanded into various fields, such as natural language processing, computer vision, robotics, and general AI. Natural language processing refers to the ability of machines to understand and generate human language, which has driven the development of virtual assistants and machine translation systems. In computer vision, AI can analyze images and videos to recognize objects, people, or situations. In robotics, AI allows robots to interact with their environment and make decisions in real time.

The evolution of AI has been driven by advances in computational role, access to large volumes of data, and the development of more sophisticated algorithms. For example, the use of graphics processing units (GPUs) has made it possible to accelerate the training of AI models, while cloud storage and processing have helped access to scalable computational resources. In addition, the availability of massive datasets has made it possible to train more correct and robust models. As technology continues to advance, AI is expected to continue to grow and play an increasingly relevant role in our society and in various industries. AI has the potential to transform sectors such as medicine, agriculture, energy and transportation, by improving efficiency, accuracy and decision-making. However, it also poses ethical and societal challenges, such as data privacy, algorithmic bias and the impact on employment.

In short, AI is a constantly evolving field that looks to develop systems capable of performing tasks that previously could only be performed by humans. Through machine learning, artificial neural networks, and other approaches, AI has made significant advances and expanded into different areas. With continuous technological progress, AI has the potential to transform our society and improve various aspects of our daily lives.

- Practical applications of AI in our daily lives

Virtual assistants, those ingenious AI programs, have been designed with the purpose of understanding and responding to our questions and voice commands in such a natural way that it feels like we are conversing with another person. These assistants make use of advanced natural language processing and machine learning techniques to interpret our requests and provide us with relevant and useful answers. In recent times, these virtual assistants have become extremely popular and are present in our mobile devices, smart speakers and other connected devices. Surely you have heard of some of them, such as Apple's Siri, Google Assistant, Amazon

Alexa and Microsoft Cortana, which have become authentic digital companions.

Virtual assistants offer us a wide range of amazing functionalities. We can ask them questions to get instant information about the weather, the latest news, traffic conditions and many other topics of interest. In addition, they make it easier for us to perform various tasks, such as setting reminders, sending messages, making phone calls, playing music and controlling the smart devices in our home.

However, the most fascinating thing about these virtual assistants is their ability to adapt and learn from our interactions. As we use them, these astute colleagues collect data about our preferences and behaviors, allowing them to further personalize our experiences. For example, if we ask the virtual assistant to play music, over time it will learn what our favorite genres and artists are, creating playlists according to our musical tastes. Also, if we ask you to suggest nearby restaurants, the assistant will learn our gastronomic preferences and recommend places that fit our tastes.

The presence of virtual assistants in our daily lives is a clear example of how AI has managed to transform the way we interact with technology. These digital companions have become true allies, always providing us with instant information and personalized help. Thanks to them, our daily activities have been simplified and our efficiency has improved significantly.

In short, virtual assistants are a splendid example of how AI has managed to completely change the way we relate to technology. Thanks to their ability to understand and respond to our requests so naturally, they have become indispensable tools in our routine, providing us with instant information and personalized aid that really is effective in our daily lives.

- How AI is transforming various industries

In the first chapter, we have explored the impact of Artificial Intelligence (AI) on various industries. Here's a detailed explanation of how AI is transforming different industries, providing practical examples of its application in each.

1. Health: AI is revolutionizing the field of medicine by improving both the diagnosis and treatment of diseases. Using machine learning algorithms, copious amounts of medical data, such as MRI images and patient records, can be analyzed. For example, radiologists can use AI to detect lesions or abnormalities in medical images more accurately and quickly. In addition, AI can help doctors develop more personalized

treatments by considering the individual characteristics of each patient.

2. Automotive: AI is transforming the automotive industry with the introduction of autonomous vehicles. These cars use AI algorithms to interpret data from sensors, such as cameras and radar, enabling real-time decision-making. For example, AI systems can detect pedestrians, vehicles and traffic signs, and thus adapt the behavior of the vehicle accordingly. This not only improves transport safety, but also its efficiency by perfecting fuel consumption and reducing traffic congestion.

3. Finance: In the financial sector, AI is employed in risk analysis, fraud detection and portfolio management. AI algorithms can analyze large

volumes of financial data in real time, finding patterns and anomalies that might go unnoticed by humans. For example, AI can detect fraudulent transactions or find investment opportunities based on the analysis of historical data. This enables financial institutions to make informed decisions, reduce risk and improve the customer experience.

4. Manufacturing: AI is present in the optimization of manufacturing processes, supply chain planning and predictive maintenance. AI systems can analyze real-time data to detect inefficiencies, predict equipment failures, and perfect production. For example, on an assembly line, AI can find patterns of errors or deviations in the process and take corrective action instantly.

This translates into reduced costs, improved product quality and greater overall efficiency.

5. E-commerce: On e-commerce platforms, AI is used to deliver personalized recommendations to customers based on their purchase history and preferences. These recommender systems use AI algorithms to analyze enormous amounts of data and supply relevant suggestions. For example, if a customer has bought related products in the past, AI can recommend other items they might be interested in. This helps users discover new products and improves their shopping experience, thus increasing online sales.

6. Energy: AI is used in the management and optimization of smart grids. AI algorithms analyze real-time data from smart meters, allowing to

forecast energy demand and perfect its distribution. For example, AI can predict energy consumption patterns based on factors such as weather, time of day, and extraordinary events. This helps a more efficient management of energy distribution, reducing costs and promoting the integration of renewable sources into the electricity grid.

These are just a few examples that illustrate how AI is transforming different industries. Overall, AI supplies opportunities to automate tasks, make data-driven decisions, and improve efficiency across multiple sectors. As technology advances, AI is expected to continue to play a pivotal role in the innovation and development of industries in the future, opening new possibilities and improving people's quality of life.

Chapter 2: Machine Learning and Algorithms

In this chapter, we'll start by highlighting the importance of machine learning in the field of AI. It is amazing to discover how machines can learn autonomously from data, without the need to be explicitly programmed. This opens a universe of possibilities, as machines can buy knowledge and skills from experience and apply them to complex tasks, such as pattern recognition, data classification and decision making.

As we delve deeper into the basics of machine learning algorithms, we discover that there are different approaches. For example, supervised learning uses labeled examples to train models, allowing machines to learn from previously classified data. On the other hand, unsupervised learning allows you to discover patterns and structures in data without labels, which can be useful for showing groupings or trends. In addition, reinforcement learning is based on the principle of reward and punishment so that machines learn to make best decisions in a specific environment.

But we will not stay only in theory, we will also examine the practical applications of machine learning, how it is used in voice recognition to interact with intelligent virtual assistants, such as Siri or Alexa, where machines can understand and respond to our questions and voice commands. It is also used in fraud detection to protect our financial transactions, naming suspicious patterns in data and preventing potential cyber-attacks. In the medical field, machine learning can aid in diagnosis, analyzing copious amounts of medical data and supporting healthcare professionals in making more correct decisions. In addition, in the business field, it is used to predict market behavior and perfect business strategies, allowing companies to expect trends and make informed decisions.

These are just a few examples that illustrate how machine learning is transforming multiple sectors and improving our quality of life. From personalizing recommendations on streaming platforms to autonomous vehicle driving, machine learning has proven its incredible ability to adapt and evolve across different domains.

Algorithms are revolutionizing the way we interact with technology and are becoming an essential tool to boost innovation in various fields. The ability of machines to learn and improve autonomously is opening new doors to a future full of possibilities.

- The role of machine learning in AI

Machine learning plays a pivotal role in the field of Artificial Intelligence (AI) as it allows machines to learn and improve their performance from data. It gives them the ability to get knowledge and make decisions based on experience.

The main idea behind machine learning is that machines can discover patterns and connections in data using special algorithms. These algorithms allow them to find important characteristics and make decisions based on them. As machines train on different data sets, they improve their models and become more skilled at specific tasks.

One of the most prominent advantages of machine learning in AI is its ability to manage substantial amounts of data. As the amount of information available increases tremendously, machine learning helps us extract valuable insights and discover patterns that might go unnoticed by us. This makes it easier for us to make more informed decisions and make more correct predictions in various areas.

In addition, machine learning could adapt and improve over time. As machines are exposed to more data and situations, their machine learning models can be updated and adjusted to be increasingly correct. This ability of constant learning allows them to face more complex challenges and learn from new experiences.

Machine learning plays an essential role in many AI applications, such as speech recognition systems, computer vision, machine translation, and recommendation systems. For example, in the field of computer vision, machine learning allows machines to recognize objects, faces, and scenes in images and videos. In the case of recommendation systems, machine learning analyzes the user's history and preferences to offer personalized suggestions for movies, products, or connections on social networks.

In short, machine learning is a key part of AI, providing us with the tools needed to teach machines to learn and improve using data. Its ability to manage large volumes of information, adapt and continuously improve makes it an essential element in the development and advancement of AI in different applications and sectors.

- Basic machine learning algorithms

In the field of Artificial Intelligence, algorithms play a crucial role in helping us extract valuable insights from available data. Below are some of the most common algorithms used in machine learning:

1. Linear regression: This algorithm allows us to understand the relationship between different variables. For example, if we want to predict the price of a house based on its size and location, we can use linear regression to find a formula that relates these variables.

2. Decision trees: Decision trees help us make decisions based on different conditions. Let's imagine that we want to determine whether some fruit is an apple, or an orange based on its shape

and color. We can use a decision tree to guide us in this process.

3. Support vector machines (SVMs): These machines help us classify objects into distinct categories. For example, if we want to separate emails into "spam" or "not spam", we can use an SVM to find the best way to make this distinction.

4. Nearest neighbors: This algorithm helps us classify objects based on their nearest neighbors. Suppose we want to decide whether a picture shows a dog or a cat. We can search for similar images in our database and use their classification to make our decision.

5. Neural networks: These algorithms are inspired by the functioning of the human brain. Neural networks consist of interconnected layers of

neurons, where each neuron performs a nonlinear transformation of the data. They are widely used in tasks such as image recognition, natural language processing, and other complex problems.

These examples are just a small sample of the basic algorithms used in machine learning. Each of them has its own strengths and weaknesses, and choosing the right algorithm depends on the problem and the specific data you are working with. In the next chapter, we will explore practical examples of machine learning applications to better understand how these algorithms are used in real-world situations.

- Examples of machine learning applications

Machine learning finds application in various fields and offers innovative solutions to many problems. Here are some practical examples of machine learning applications:

1. Facial recognition: Machine learning is used in facial recognition systems that allow people to be found and authenticated through their face. These systems are used in security, access control and in personalized marketing applications. For example, many social media apps use facial recognition to tag people in photos.

2. Machine translation: Machine learning algorithms are applied in machine translation systems that allow translating text from one language to another efficiently and accurately.

These systems have experienced a breakthrough in recent years, easing effective communication between people who speak different languages. A famous example is Google's translation service.

3. Chatbots: Chatbots are virtual assistants that use machine learning to interact with users and supply automatic answers and solutions to usual questions. They are found in different industries, such as customer service, technical support, and sales. For example, many websites use a chatbot to answer queries and supply immediate aid to users.

4. Sentiment analysis: Machine learning is used to analyze and understand opinions and emotions expressed in text, such as social media comments or product reviews. This helps companies gain

valuable insights into public opinion and make informed decisions based on it. For example, many companies use sentiment analysis to assess customer satisfaction.

5. Recommendation systems: Machine learning algorithms are used on streaming platforms, e-commerce and social networks to offer personalized recommendations to users. These systems analyze user behavior and preferences to suggest relevant content, products, or connections. A popular example of a recommendation system is the one used by Netflix to suggest movies and series to its subscribers.

These examples illustrate how machine learning is applied in different areas, improving efficiency and user experience. Its ability to process data, detect patterns and make decisions based on them has transformed various fields, opening new possibilities in AI and generating significant advances in different sectors.

Chapter 3: Neural Networks and Deep Learning

In this chapter ahead, we will learn about two fundamental pillars in the field of Artificial Intelligence, neural networks, and deep learning, which have driven important revolutionary advances in various areas of knowledge and have captured the attention of researchers and AI enthusiasts around the world.

Let's start by exploring in detail the workings of neural networks, these powerful tools inspired by the human brain and its ability to process information. Using a structure composed of interconnected neurons, neural networks can conduct complex calculations and extract patterns from data. We will reveal the ins and outs of neural connections and how electrical and chemical signals are transmitted throughout the network.

Once we have understood the basic architecture of neural networks, we will learn about deep learning, a technique that allows neural networks to learn autonomously through training with large volumes of data. We will examine the diverse types of deep learning, such as supervised, unsupervised, and reinforcement, and understand how they apply in various scenarios.

One of the most exciting aspects of deep learning is its ability to perform impressive tasks. For example, neural networks can be trained to recognize images, which has led to significant advances in fields such as computer vision and robotics. In addition, they are used in natural language processing, allowing machines to understand and generate text more accurately and naturally. These are just a few examples of how deep learning is transforming the way we interact with technology.

As we explore the key concepts and practical applications of these techniques, we will understand how they are revolutionizing Artificial Intelligence and shaping the future of technology. We are seeing an unprecedented advance in the ability of machines to learn and adapt, opening a range of exciting possibilities in fields as diverse as medicine, scientific research, autonomous driving and much more. Deep learning is leading us into a new era of technological discovery and advancement, and it is imperative to be prepared

to harness its full potential.

- Fundamentals of neural networks

Neural networks, inspired by the functioning of the human brain, have become powerful tools in the field of Artificial Intelligence. Some basic concepts are:

1. Artificial Neurons: We can think of artificial neurons as the fundamental elements of neural networks. Like neurons in our brain, these artificial neurons receive information, process it, and generate a response. For example, suppose we want to develop a handwritten digit recognition system. Each artificial neuron could receive information about the pixels in an image and process it to decide whether it stands for a specific number.

2. Connections and Weights: Neurons in a neural network are connected to each other. Each connection has a weight that decides the importance of one neuron in relation to the others. During network training, these weights are adjusted to improve your performance. In the digit recognition example, connections and weights would stand for the strength of synaptic connections between artificial neurons. These weights would be adjusted so that the network learns to recognize the different digits more accurately.

3. Layers: Neurons are grouped into layers within a neural network. The input layer receives the first information, the hidden layers process that information, and the output layer produces the

results. Each layer contributes to the network's learning and decision-making process. In the case of digit recognition, we could have an input layer that receives the pixels from the image, one or several hidden layers that extract relevant characteristics from the digits, and an output layer that shows the recognized number.

4. Activation Functions: Each neuron applies an activation function to decide whether to activate based on the inputs received. These functions allow the network to learn complex patterns and relationships in the data. In digit recognition, an activation function could decide whether the weighted sum of pixels in the image exceeds a certain threshold, thereby activating the neuron associated with a specific number.

5. Learning: During training, the neural network learns from examples with known labels. The network output is compared to the desired output and the weights of the connections are adjusted to minimize the difference. This allows the network to improve its performance over time. For example, in digit recognition, images of digits with their labels corresponding to the network would be presented. If the network produces an incorrect output, the weights of the connections would be adjusted to reduce the error and improve the accuracy of recognition.

These fundamental concepts of neural networks will lay the foundation for implementing and using neural networks in various AI applications in the coming chapters.

- The concept of deep learning

Deep learning is an advanced technique that allows neural networks to tackle more complex problems and make more sophisticated decisions. Let's look at the key aspects of deep learning:

1. Deep Layers: In deep learning, neural networks have multiple internal layers that allow them to learn more deeply and capture complex features of data. Imagine a facial recognition system using deep learning. The inner layers of the network could learn simpler features, such as lines and edges, in the lower layers, and combine those features to recognize more complex facial features in the upper layers.

2. Automatic Feature Extraction: Deep learning allows neural networks to automatically learn the

most relevant features of data, without needing to be explicitly told what to look for. In facial recognition, deep learning would allow the neural network to automatically show the distinctive features of a human face, such as eyes, nose and mouth, without requiring specific manual programming for each feature.

3. Powerful Models: Deep learning allows neural networks to become larger and more complex, allowing them to oversee large volumes of information and learn more detailed patterns. In speech recognition, deep learning makes it possible to train neural networks with millions of speech examples, allowing them to capture subtle patterns and improve the accuracy of voice transcription.

4. Level Learning: Deep learning takes advantage of the idea of learning at levels, where the lower layers of the network learn simpler features and the upper layers combine those features to form more complex representations. For example, in machine translation, the first layers of a neural network could learn to translate individual words, while the upper layers would learn to combine those words into grammatically correct structures.

5. Practical Applications: Deep learning has had a major impact in many areas, such as computer vision, speech recognition, machine translation, and virtual assistants. It is present in technologies such as facial recognition, recommendation systems and autonomous vehicles.

Today, deep learning is used to show objects in images, translate text in real time, and enable natural interactions with virtual assistants, such as chatbots.

In the next chapters, we will delve into real cases and practical examples to better understand how this technique is transforming the way we interact with technology.

- Deep Learning Use Cases Today

Deep learning is applied in various fields with impressive results. Here are some use cases for deep learning today:

1. Image Recognition: Deep learning has revolutionized image recognition, allowing machines to find and classify objects in photographs or videos. This applies in applications such as face detection, object identification, and automatic image tagging. For example, neural networks trained with deep learning can automatically recognize whether an image holds a dog or cat, making it easier to organize and search for images in photo management applications.

2. Natural Language Processing: Deep learning is used to improve the understanding and generation of natural language by machines. It is applied in tasks such as speech recognition, machine translation, text generation, and chatbots. An example of deep learning application in natural language processing is machine translation, where neural networks can learn to translate text between different languages without requiring specific grammar rules.

3. Autonomous Driving: Deep learning is fundamental in the development of autonomous vehicles. It allows cars to learn to recognize traffic signs, show pedestrians and other vehicles, and make safe driving decisions. Autonomous driving systems use neural networks trained with deep

learning to interpret data from sensors, such as cameras and radar, and make real-time decisions to keep safe and efficient driving.

4. Medicine and Health: Deep learning is transforming the field of medicine by aiding in medical diagnosis, disease research, and personalization of treatments. It is used to analyze medical images, detect abnormalities in X-rays and MRIs, and predict disease risk. For example, neural networks trained with deep learning can help detect cancer early on mammography images, easing more correct and prompt diagnosis.

5. Finance: Deep learning is used in financial data analysis to detect fraud, predict market movements and improve investment decision-making. It is also applied in the improvement of

the customer experience in financial services, through the personalization of recommendations and offers. In the financial realm, neural networks trained with deep learning can analyze large volumes of historical and real-time data to find patterns and trends that help make informed decisions in stock investment or detection of fraudulent activity.

These are just a few examples of how deep learning is being applied today. Its potential is enormous, and it is driving significant advances in various fields, improving our daily lives and opening up new opportunities in research and technological development.

Get ready to continue exploring the fascinating world of deep learning in the following chapters!

Chapter 4: Natural Language Processing

In Chapter 4, we will explore how machines can understand and process human language efficiently and accurately. This discipline is fundamental in the field of Artificial Intelligence since it allows us to interact with machines in a natural and fluid way.

We'll start by understanding what exactly natural language processing is and how it has come to form an integral part of our everyday lives. We will study how machines can analyze and understand human language, and how these capabilities are revolutionizing the way we interact with technology. For example, consider a speech recognition system that uses natural language processing. Through advanced algorithms, the machine can automatically transcribe speech into text, making it easier to find and organize information in transcription applications or virtual assistants.

In the techniques and algorithms used in natural language processing, we will explore everything from basic text preprocessing to more advanced language models, which allow us to perform tasks such as machine translation, text generation, and sentiment classification. For example, language models based on neural networks, such as GPT-4, can generate coherent and relevant text from a small first input. These models are used in applications such as chatbots, where they can supply personalized answers to users' questions quickly and effectively.

We will explore the applications of natural language processing in chatbots and virtual assistants. We will discover how these technologies are transforming our interaction with online services and applications, supplying fast and personalized answers to our questions and needs. For example, chatbots use natural language processing techniques to understand and respond to user queries in real time. These systems can help in customer support, supply information about products or services, and even supply personalized recommendations based on user preferences.

In short, this chapter is a comprehensive guide to understanding the world of natural language processing. Get ready to explore the fundamentals of human-machine communication and discover the endless possibilities that natural language processing has to offer.

- What is natural language processing?

If you've ever wondered how computers can understand and process human language similarly to us, you're about to find out. Natural language processing is a branch of artificial intelligence that focuses on teaching machines to understand and communicate in human language. It aims to train computers to analyze, interpret and generate text in an analogous way as a person would.

This involves machines being able to understand the meaning of words, recognize the grammar and structure of sentences, and grasp the context and intent behind a message. Natural language processing is used in a wide variety of practical applications, such as virtual assistants, machine translation, social sentiment analysis, chatbots, and custom recommendation systems. Its aim is to ease the interaction between humans and machines, allowing a more natural and effective communication.

For example, consider a virtual assistant that uses natural language processing. This assistant can understand and respond to voice commands such as "Turn on the lights" or "Play my favorite song." The machine interprets human language and executes corresponding actions, supplying a more intuitive and convenient experience for the user.

- Techniques and algorithms used in natural language processing

Natural language processing uses a variety of techniques and algorithms to enable machines to understand and work with human language effectively. These techniques cover various aspects of text processing, allowing for deeper analysis and better understanding of language.

One of the common techniques is syntactic analysis, which focuses on finding the grammatical structure of a sentence, such as subject, verb, and complements. This helps machines understand how words relate to each other in a sentence.

Another important technique is semantic analysis, which looks to understand the meaning of words and their relationship in the context of a larger sentence or text. This involves understanding the intention behind the words and grasping the meaning beyond literal interpretation.

In addition, classification and grouping algorithms are used to organize and categorize large volumes of text based on topics or similar characteristics. This is especially useful in tasks such as sentiment analysis in social networks, where you want to decide if a text has a positive, negative or neutral connotation. Named entity recognition algorithms are also used, which allow finding and extracting relevant information, such as names of people, places and dates, from a text. This is useful in applications such as news processing or legal document analysis.

In addition, techniques such as tagging parts of sentences, disambiguation of polysemic words and automatic digests are all contributing to improving the ability of machines to understand and generate text.

For example, if we are developing a customer support chatbot, we could use natural language processing techniques to analyze user queries and supply relevant and useful answers in real time. The chatbot could understand the context and intent behind the customer's questions and respond appropriately and accurately.

- Applications of natural language processing (NLP) in chatbots and virtual assistants

Applications of natural language processing in chatbots and virtual assistants are transforming the way we interact with machines and how we get information and help.

Natural language processing enables chatbots and virtual assistants to understand and respond to human language intelligently. This means they can understand what we say or write to them and supply relevant answers.

Imagine having a fluid conversation with a chatbot as if you were talking to a real person. You can ask questions, request information, and receive understandable and helpful answers. This is possible thanks to natural language processing, which allows these tools to analyze the text we supply them and understand its meaning.

Chatbots and virtual assistants use natural language processing techniques and algorithms to process human language. They can recognize keywords, understand the context of a conversation, and learn from earlier interactions to improve their responses. This makes communication with them more natural and fluid. These applications of natural language processing are used in a wide range of cases, from online customer support to personalized recommendations. Chatbots can help you book flights, make purchases, learn about products and services, and more. Virtual assistants, such as Siri or Alexa, allow you to control your home devices, get news and access useful information simply by talking to them.

In short, natural language processing has revolutionized the way we interact with technology through chatbots and virtual assistants. These apps give us fast, personalized answers, simplify our daily tasks, and make our lives easier. Natural language processing continues to evolve and open new possibilities in the field of artificial intelligence and human-machine communication.

Chapter 5: Computer Vision

Computer vision, a discipline that aims to teach machines to see and understand images and videos similarly to us humans. In recent years, computer vision has experienced amazing advances and has transformed many areas of our daily lives, opening endless possibilities.

Computer vision is based on the development and application of techniques and algorithms that allow machines to process and analyze visual information efficiently. Its main purpose is to equip computers with the ability to understand the content of images, which involves finding objects, recognizing patterns, and performing complex tasks such as motion tracking, face detection, and object classification.

In this chapter, we will examine the fundamental concepts of computer vision, how images are processed, relevant features are extracted, and essential elements in a visual scene are found and separated. In addition, we will recognize the algorithms and techniques most used in this discipline, including pattern recognition, machine learning and convolutional neural networks, which have proven to be especially effective in the analysis of images and videos.

We will give outstanding examples of success in the field of computer vision and how this discipline has had a positive impact in areas as diverse as medicine, security, manufacturing and augmented reality, among other sectors.

We will know concrete cases of successful applications, such as facial recognition in security systems, the precise identification of objects in the industry and advanced help in medical surgeries.

It is worth noting that computer vision faces significant challenges, such as the ability to deal with several types of images, real-time detection of moving objects, and understanding complex contexts. However, technological advances and constant research are driving progress in this field, allowing the development of increasingly exact and efficient systems.

We will understand from the identification of objects in photographs to the analysis of videos to ensure safety, this discipline is constantly evolving and presents incredible potential to improve and ease various aspects of our modern world. Thanks to computer vision, new opportunities open for task automation, process optimization and the creation of more immersive and enriching visual experiences.

- Computer Vision Basics

Computer vision is a fascinating discipline that looks to equip machines with the ability to understand and process visual information, like how we humans do. It is based on the development of algorithms and techniques that allow computers to analyze and understand images and videos.

At its most basic level, computer vision involves processing images to extract relevant features, such as borders, colors, and textures. These features are then used to perform more complex tasks, such as object detection, facial recognition, and image classification.

To achieve this, algorithms are used that can find patterns in images and learn to recognize different objects and visual elements. These algorithms are trained on datasets having labeled images, that is, images accompanied by information about the objects or features they hold.

Computer vision has many practical applications in our daily lives. For example, it is used in security systems for facial recognition and detection of suspicious behavior. It is also applied in the manufacturing industry for the quality inspection of products and in medicine for the diagnosis of diseases from medical images.

As research in the field of computer vision advances, more advanced techniques are being developed, such as the use of convolutional neural networks, which mimic the way the human brain processes visual information. This has allowed for more correct and sophisticated results in tasks such as naming objects in complex images and segmenting specific elements in a scene.

In short, computer vision is an exciting discipline that looks to enable machines to understand and analyze visual information, such as images and videos. It uses algorithms and techniques to process and extract relevant features from images, enabling tasks such as object recognition and scene analysis to be performed. This technology has practical applications in various fields, from security to medicine and manufacturing.

- Algorithms and techniques used in computer vision

In computer vision, various algorithms and techniques are used to process and analyze images to extract meaningful information. These algorithms and techniques are applied to perform tasks such as object detection, facial recognition, image classification, and segmentation of elements in an image.

One of the most used algorithms in computer vision is the feature detection algorithm, which looks for specific patterns in an image. These features can include borders, corners, textures, or regions of interest. By finding these features, tasks such as object detection or facial recognition can be performed.

Another widely used algorithm is the classification algorithm, which allows to tag or categorize images into different classes or categories. These algorithms are trained on pre-labeled datasets, allowing them to learn to recognize and classify new images.

As for the techniques, one of the most used is the use of filters, which allow to highlight certain characteristics of an image and cut noise or imperfections. Segmentation techniques are also employed, which consist of dividing an image into smaller regions or finding specific areas of interest.

In addition, more advanced techniques based on deep learning, such as convolutional neural networks, are being developed. These neural networks are designed to learn to recognize patterns and features in images in ways like the human brain. Thanks to their ability to learn and adapt, these neural networks can achieve exact results in complex computer vision tasks.

In summary, computer vision uses algorithms and techniques to process images and extract relevant information. These algorithms can detect features, classify images, and perform other specific tasks. In addition, more advanced techniques based on deep learning, such as convolutional neural networks, are being explored, which allow more precise and sophisticated results in image analysis.

- Success stories in the field of computer vision

Computer vision has had many success stories in various fields, where it has been successfully applied to solve problems and improve processes. Here are some highlights:

1. Facial recognition in security systems: Facial recognition technology has advanced considerably thanks to computer vision. Currently, it is used in security applications, such as face unlock on mobile devices or the identification of people in surveillance cameras. It is also used in social networks to automatically tag people in photos.

2. Autonomous vehicles: Computer vision plays a crucial role in autonomous vehicles. Using advanced cameras and algorithms, these vehicles

can detect and recognize traffic signs, pedestrians, vehicles and obstacles in real time. This enables safe and efficient autonomous driving.

3. Quality control in manufacturing industry: Computer vision is used to inspect the quality of products in manufacturing industry. Algorithms can show defects, such as cracks, imperfections or deviations in shape or color, thus ensuring that products meet the required quality standards.

4. Medicine and health: Computer vision has found applications in the medical field, such as in the early detection of diseases. For example, algorithms capable of analyzing medical images, such as X-rays or MRIs, have been developed to name abnormalities and aid in the diagnosis of diseases.

5. Precision agriculture: Computer vision is used in agriculture to perfect crop yield. Drones equipped with cameras and computer vision algorithms can be used to find areas with diseases or pests, enabling precise pesticide application and minimizing environmental impact.

These are just a few examples of the many success stories in the field of computer vision. Continuous research and advances in this discipline promise a future full of innovative and beneficial applications in different sectors.

Chapter 6: Ethics in Artificial Intelligence

Ethics in artificial intelligence (AI) is a discipline in constant progress that plays an increasingly relevant role in society. As AI continues to transform various aspects of our lives, it is essential to take a detailed look at the ethical challenges associated with its development and application.

AI, being able to process a lot of information and conduct thinking tasks, makes us ask ethical questions that we must consider. Some of these dilemmas relate to data privacy and security, algorithmic discrimination, accountability of autonomous systems, and transparency in AI decision-making processes. In addition, AI raises ethical questions in fields such as the automation of jobs, the fair distribution of benefits, and the preservation of human autonomy.

During our exploration, we will analyze the essential aspects in the development and ethical use of AI. We will reflect on fairness and bias prevention in algorithms, as well as the importance of being transparent and accountable in the design and operation of AI systems. We will also address ethics in data collection and use, as well as the need to set up right regulatory frameworks to guide the development and implementation of AI.

In this sense, it is crucial to understand that the goal is not to slow down the progress of AI, but to ensure that it is used responsibly and beneficial to the well-being of society. We will look to find a balance between technological innovation and the protection of moral values and human rights.

As we move forward in our exploration, it is critical to consider that ethics in AI is an ever-evolving process. Discussions and debates on these issues must be ongoing and adapt as new challenges and technological advances arise. Collaboration between experts in AI, law and society needs to be fostered to effectively address moral dilemmas and set up guidelines to guide the responsible application of AI.

In summary, this chapter invites us to reflect on the moral challenges that go with the development and use of AI. Only through a thoughtful approach can we harness the potential of AI and

ensure that it contributes positively and
responsibly to our world.

- The ethical challenges associated with AI

Artificial Intelligence (AI) confronts us with important ethical challenges that we must address responsibly. As this technology advances, fundamental questions arise about how it will affect society and how it will respect our ethical values. It's important to understand these challenges, even if we're not familiar with AI. Let's look at some of the most relevant challenges:

1. Algorithmic bias: One of the most important ethical challenges is algorithmic bias. This means that AI systems can generate unfair or discriminatory results due to biases present in the data they were trained on. For example, if an AI system is used to select candidates for a job and training data is biased towards a certain group, that

86

group will be unfairly favored and others will be excluded, perpetuating inequalities and discrimination.

2. Privacy and data protection: Another crucial ethical challenge is privacy and data protection. AI systems require a large amount of personal information to function properly, raising concerns about how that data is collected, stored and used. It is essential to ensure the confidentiality and security of personal information to prevent possible abuses and protect individual rights. For example, ensuring that data is stored securely, and that proper consent is obtained before using it.

3. Transparency in decision-making: The lack of transparency in the algorithms used by AI systems can lead to mistrust and make accountability

difficult in case of mistakes or negative consequences. It is crucial to understand how decisions are arrived at and what factors are considered. For example, in the field of justice, if an AI system is used to make sentencing decisions, it is essential to know how the data was considered and what criteria were used.

4. Responsibility and accountability: As AI systems become more autonomous and independent, we need to prove clear mechanisms to decide who oversees the decisions made by these systems and how to deal with potential mistakes or negative consequences. Lack of clarity in this regard can have significant ethical implications. For example, in the case of

autonomous vehicles, who is liable in case of an accident caused by the AI system?

5. Automation of jobs and fair distribution of benefits: It is important to consider the impact of AI on the workplace and the fair distribution of benefits. While AI can automate certain jobs, it can also create new opportunities and skills. However, it is crucial to ensure that the implementation of AI is fair and does not generate inequalities. For example, if job automation disproportionately affects certain sectors or groups of the population, measures must be taken to mitigate this impact and ensure a just transition.

In short, the ethical challenges associated with AI are many and complex. They require careful reflection and responsible implementation of this technology. We must address algorithmic bias, protect privacy and personal data, ensure transparency in decisions made by AI systems, prove clear mechanisms of responsibility and accountability, and ensure a fair distribution of benefits. In addressing these ethical challenges, we look to ensure that AI is developed and used ethically, promoting the benefit and well-being of all society. Throughout history, humans have proved a remarkable ability to adapt to technological changes and find ways to harness them to our advantage. AI is no different. While it poses ethical challenges, it also presents opportunities to improve our lives and promote progress. By understanding and addressing these ethical challenges, we can use AI responsibly and work towards a future where technology and humans work together to achieve common goals.

- Important considerations in the development and use of AI systems

When we talk about the development and use of Artificial Intelligence (AI), there are fundamental ethical and practical aspects that we must consider. As we move forward in the implementation of this technology, it is particularly important to address these aspects responsibly and consciously. Here are some important things to consider:

1. Transparency: One of the fundamental aspects in the development and use of AI systems is transparency. AI systems need to be transparent about how they work and how they make decisions. This involves understanding how results are obtained and what factors are

considered when making decisions. Transparency helps build trust and makes it possible to assess whether decisions made by AI systems are fair and impartial. For example, in the case of recommendation systems used on e-commerce platforms, it is important for users to understand how recommendations are generated and what data is used.

2. Ethics in data collection and use: AI systems require a lot of data to learn and make decisions. However, it is important that data collection and use are done ethically. This involves respecting people's privacy, obtaining their consent to use their data, and making sure there is no bias or bias in the datasets used. For example, when training an AI system to recognize images, it is important

to use a diverse and representative dataset to avoid bias or discrimination.

3. Responsibility and accountability: In the development and use of AI systems, it is essential to set up clear mechanisms of responsibility and accountability. This involves deciding who manages the decisions made by AI systems and how potential errors or negative consequences can be corrected. Responsibility and accountability are shared between developers, AI providers and end users.

. For example, in the case of autonomous vehicles, it is necessary to prove who assumes responsibility in case of accidents or incidents.

4. Social and economic impact: The implementation of AI systems can have a

significant impact on society and the economy. It is important to consider how it affects employment, inequality and the distribution of resources. Steps must be taken to ensure that AI is used fairly and equitably, avoiding excessive concentration of power and ensuring that the benefits are widely distributed. For example, it is necessary to consider how AI-driven automation can affect certain labor sectors and look for alternatives to ensure the employability of people.

5. Continuous evaluation and improvement: AI systems must be constantly evaluated to ensure they are effective, efficient and ethical. Feedback and learning mechanisms should be implemented to continually improve these systems, correct any biases or errors they may have, and adapt them as

new ethical concerns arise. For example, organizations using AI systems should conduct regular audits to assess the fairness and reliability of the results generated. In summary, the development and use of AI requires us to consider important aspects such as transparency, ethics in data collection and use, responsibility and accountability, social and economic impact, and continuous evaluation. By paying attention to these aspects, we look to ensure that AI is developed and used ethically and responsibly, maximizing its benefits and minimizing its risks.

- Reflections on the ethical future of AI

AI is a powerful technology that is transforming our society, and it is important to consider the ethical aspects that arise with its advancement. While AI can offer significant benefits, it also poses challenges that we must address responsibly.

First, AI transparency is a crucial issue to consider. AI systems can make complex decisions that affect our lives, such as in the field of medicine or justice. To trust these decisions, it is necessary to understand how they are arrived at and what factors are considered. Transparency helps us assess whether the results are fair, impartial and ethical. For example, in the medical field, if an AI system recommends a treatment, it is critical that healthcare professionals understand the reasoning behind that recommendation.

Another point to consider is privacy and data use in AI. AI systems require enormous amounts of data to learn and improve their performance. However, it is critical to ensure that personal data is used ethically, and that people's privacy is protected. This involves obtaining proper consent to use the data and ensuring that it is oversaw securely and confidentially. For example, companies that collect user data must ensure that they follow privacy regulations and use security measures to protect information.

Fairness and justice are also crucial ethical considerations in the development and use of AI. We must ensure that the implementation of AI does not widen existing inequalities in society. This involves avoiding bias and discrimination in the algorithms used, as well as ensuring a fair distribution of the benefits of AI. For example, if AI is used in hiring processes, it is necessary to ensure that algorithms do not favor certain groups and exclude others unfairly.

Responsibility and accountability are also key elements in the ethical future of AI. We must set up clear mechanisms to figure out who manages the decisions made by AI systems and how to deal with errors or negative consequences. In addition, it is important to develop regulations and ethical standards that guide the development and use of AI. The creation of ethics committees, audits and review mechanisms can help ensure that AI is used responsibly, and risks are minimized.

In conclusion, the ethical future of AI depends on how we address challenges and consider core values. We must promote transparency, protect privacy, ensure fairness and justice, and show mechanisms of responsibility and accountability. If we work together to develop and use AI ethically, we can harness its full potential to improve our quality of life and move forward as a society.

Summary:

Throughout this book, we've had the opportunity to explore how artificial intelligence (AI) is transforming our lives in surprising ways and opening up a world full of opportunities. When delving into the subject of AI, it is common to feel some apprehension or fear towards this emerging technology. However, it is important to remember that AI does not look to replace us, but to complement and help us become better at what we do.

Let's imagine for a moment that we live in a time when machines don't exist. Our work and daily activities would require much more time and effort. AI allows us to do tasks more efficiently and accurately, freeing us up to engage in activities that require more creativity, ethical thinking, and empathy.

Throughout history, technological advances have been part of our development as human beings. From the invention of the wheel to the industrial revolution, we have seen changes that at the time could generate uncertainty, but that in the long term have allowed us to achieve unprecedented levels of progress and well-being.

The advent of AI stands for another milestone in this evolution. AI gives us skills and capabilities that we only dreamed of before. Thanks to AI, we can tackle complex problems more efficiently and find innovative solutions. From manufacturing to medicine and education, AI is transforming various areas of our lives, improving the productivity and quality of the services we receive. It's natural to feel fear or worry about the unknown, but it's important to understand that AI doesn't have malicious intentions or seek to replace us as human beings. Rather, it gives us tools to enhance our capabilities and overcome challenges together.

AI is a tool that helps us simplify tedious and repetitive tasks, allowing us to focus on what really matters: being creative, collaborating, and solving the complex challenges we face as a society.

Instead of fearing AI, we must learn to use it responsibly and ethically. This involves understanding its limitations, watching its development and ensuring that it is applied for the benefit of society. It is the responsibility of all of us, as individuals and as a community, to guide the path of AI towards a future where machines and humans work together to achieve common goals. In short, AI is not a cause for fear, but an opportunity to evolve and grow as a society. By understanding that AI gives us new tools and skills, we can embrace it and harness its benefits to improve our quality of life and reach unprecedented levels of progress. The key is in the collaboration between humans and machines, taking advantage of the best of both worlds to build a promising future full of possibilities.

Glossary

Welcome to the glossary of artificial intelligence terms! The purpose of this glossary is to supply a clear and concise understanding of the fundamental concepts related to artificial intelligence. As you explore these terms, you'll be able to familiarize yourself with the basics of AI and gain a broader view of this fascinating field. Whether you're a beginner in AI or just want to refresh your knowledge, this glossary will help you understand key terms, from algorithms and models to machine learning techniques and practical applications of AI. Immerse yourself in this universe of knowledge and enjoy your journey through the essential concepts of artificial intelligence. Below, you will find a glossary of words related to Artificial Intelligence and their meanings:

- **AI Ethics**: Consideration of moral values and societal implications in the development and use of AI systems.

- **Algorithm:** A set of instructions or rules that allow machines to process and solve problems.

- **Anomaly detection:** An AI technique that names unusual or atypical patterns in datasets.

- **Artificial neuron:** Basic element of an artificial neural network that performs calculations and transmits signals.

- **Automation:** Use of AI to perform tasks autonomously without human intervention.

- **Autonomous robots**: Machines with the ability to make decisions and perform actions independently using AI techniques.

- **Autonomy:** AI devices apply the term "autonomous" when they don't need help from people; that autonomy is classified into different levels. Autonomous cars, for example, reach a level 4 of autonomy when they do not need a person to use at full capacity and therefore do not have a steering wheel or pedals.

- **Big data:** Massive set of data that is analyzed to obtain valuable insights.

- **Chatbot:** AI program designed to simulate a human conversation through text or voice messages.

- **ChatGPT:** It is a language model based on artificial intelligence developed by OpenAI. It uses natural language processing technology to generate responses and hold conversations with users. ChatGPT can understand and generate coherent and relevant text on a variety of topics. It has been trained on a wide range of data and can be used to answer questions, aid or generate written content. It is a useful tool in chatbot applications, virtual assistants and automated text generation.

- **Classification:** An AI technique that organizes data into categories or groups based on similar characteristics.

- **Cloud computing**: Infrastructure that allows the storage and processing of data on remote servers, accessible through the internet.

- **Cognitive computing**: A field of AI that looks to mimic the way humans process information and make decisions.

- **Computer vision**: A field of AI that allows machines to perceive, analyze, and understand the visual environment as a human would.

- **Computer vision:** A field of AI that enables machines to understand, analyze, and extract information from images and videos.

- **Cross-validation**: A technique used in machine learning to evaluate the performance of a model on data sets other than training.

- **Cybersecurity**: Set of techniques and measures used to protect systems and data from possible threats and cyber-attacks.

- **Data labeling**: The process of assigning labels or categories to data to train AI models and improve their accuracy.

- **Data mining**: The process of exploring large data sets to discover patterns, trends, or relevant information.

- **Data privacy**: Protection and control of personal information stored and processed by AI systems.

- **Data processing**: Manipulation and transformation of data using algorithms and AI techniques to obtain relevant information.

- **Data Science**: A discipline that uses methods and techniques to extract knowledge and understand data.

- **Decision making:** The ability of machines to analyze information and select the best choice among different alternatives.

- **Deep learning**: It is the result of the work of a neural network that allows artificial intelligence to go beyond understanding what something is, but also understand why it happens.

- **Deepfakes:** Fake multimedia content created by artificial intelligence to alter videos, images or audios, changing the appearance or voice of one person for that of another.

- **Expert systems**: AI programs that mimic a human expert's ability to solve problems and make decisions.

- **Exponential growth**: A phenomenon in which the ability and performance of AI systems increase rapidly over time.

- **Extracting knowledge**: The process of discovering valuable information or meaningful patterns in large data sets.

- **Facial recognition**: An AI technique that detects and verifies the facial features of individuals.

- **Generalization:** The ability of an AI model to apply learned knowledge in new situations or similar problems.

- **Innovation:** Application of AI to develop creative and disruptive solutions in different sectors and areas.

- **Internet of Things**: Connecting physical devices to the internet to collect and share data, enabling interaction with AI systems.

- **Internet search**: Using AI algorithms to find relevant information on the web from keywords or queries.

- **Learning transfer**: AI can store the knowledge bought when solving a problem and then use it to solve another situation, different but related to the first case.

- **Machine learning**: The ability of machines to learn from data and improve its performance without being explicitly programmed.

– **Natural Language Processing**: A field of AI that deals with the interaction between humans and machines through human language.

– **Natural Language**: A form of communication used by humans in their everyday speech and writing. AI models can learn on their own, without having to feed them predefined structures. They use layers and layers of unstructured information, process the data, prove the relationships between them and find a pattern in them.

– **Neural network:** Similar in design to the human nervous system and brain, a neural network organizes learning stages to give AI the ability to solve complex problems by dividing them into data tiers. Neural networks apply the tactic of splitting into smaller data sets to overcome each layer of their learning.

- **Object Recognition**: An AI technique that shows and classifies objects in images or videos.

- **Optimization:** The process of tweaking and improving AI models and algorithms for better results.

- **Personal assistant**: An AI program or device designed to aid users in everyday tasks, such as reminders or searching for information.

- **Predictive models**: AI algorithms that use historical data to make estimates or predict future outcomes.

- **Pront:** Artificial intelligence platform developed by OpenAI. It is an advanced text generation system that allows users to get complete and consistent answers from questions or instructions given. Using natural language technology. It's a powerful tool for content creation, writing assistance, and getting accurate information. Pront has been trained on a wide variety of data and is constantly updated to improve its responsiveness and accuracy.

- **Recommendation systems:** AI algorithms that suggest relevant products, services, or content based on user preferences and behaviors.

- **Reinforcement learning**: It involves giving AI a goal that is not defined with a specific metric but requires finding a solution or improving efficiency. Instead of finding a specific answer, the AI will run various hypotheses and report the results to evaluate and adjust the following assumptions.

- **Robotics:** A field that combines AI with engineering to develop robots with cognitive abilities and physical capabilities.

- **Segmentation**: An AI technique that divides data sets into smaller, more homogeneous groups or segments.

- **Smart cities:** Application of AI and technology in the management and optimization of urban services, such as transport and energy.

- **Social networks:** Online platforms that allow users to interact and share information through AI.

- **Speech recognition**: AI technology that enables machines to understand and process human speech.

- **Supervised learning**: In the AI model, the correct answer is provided in advance: the AI knows both the question and the answer. This method of preparation is the most common because it defines the question-and-answer models by offering the greatest amount of data.

- **Supervised:** A type of machine learning where training data is provided with known tags or responses.

- **Training**: The process of teaching a machine using data to improve its performance on specific tasks.

- **Unsupervised learning**: AI models can learn on their own, without having to feed them predefined structures. They use layers and layers of unstructured information, process the data, set up the relationships between them and find a pattern in them.

- **User Experience**: A design aspect that focuses on creating intuitive and satisfying interactions between users and AI interfaces.

- **User interface:** A means through which users interact with AI systems, such as touch screens or voice commands.

- **Virtual assistant**: Program or application that interacts with users verbally or in writing to supply information or perform tasks.

- **Virtual Reality**: Technology that creates an immersive experience in a simulated environment using computer-generated graphics and sounds.

"On the horizon of artificial intelligence, there are no limits to what we can achieve. Let's harness their power to imagine, innovate and transform our world, building a future where human ingenuity and machine wisdom merge in a symphony of limitless possibilities."

Luis Angel Perez

www.ingramcontent.com/pod-product-compliance
Lightning Source LLC
LaVergne TN
LVHW051247050326
832903LV00028B/2629